12 STEP WORKBOOK

The questions in this workbook are my own version of similar questions that are used by members of various 12 step fellowships. I will be forever grateful for the knowledge and wisdom that is passed on by those who went before us.

A free printable PDF version of the questions, for use by individuals in their own recovery, is available on my website at
https://jobimia.wixsite.com/podencopress/12stepworkbook

HOW TO USE THE WORKBOOK

Welcome to your Workbook!

This Workbook is not intended to be limited to one specific addiction, whether it be substance based (like drugs, alcohol, food, solvents, prescription medication, cigarettes, etc.) or behaviour based (like sex, love, shopping, gambling, gaming, exercise and even codependency).

It is intended to be useful for members of all types of 12 step fellowships, and for those (like me) who have multiple addictions. For that reason, the questions are intentionally worded as broadly as possible.

If you are a member of more than one 12 step fellowship and find yourself running out of space to write about your experiences in all your different addictions (like me), then just grab a sheet of paper and keep writing!

The Workbook is split into three sections, the first provides a framework for working the 12 steps, the second is a short section for writing a gratitude list, and finally, at the end, there are journal pages which can be used for a multitude of purposes.

The following pages explains how to use each of the Workbook sections.

12 STEP QUESTIONS & WORKBOOK

This section is split into 12 parts; one for each step.

There is a summary at the beginning of each step section briefly explaining the step's purpose and giving you an idea of how to approach it. Your sponsor will be able to give you more guidance.

The summary page is intentionally non-religious. If you are atheist or agnostic, we suggest you use the program and the people in it as your Higher Power for the purpose of taking the steps. If you already have your own concept of a Higher Power, you are, of course, welcome to use that as your Higher Power when working the steps.

The summary page is followed by a page for listing the actions you have already completed to prepare you for taking this step. This is not a test 😃 it is intended to reassure you of your readiness.

The remaining pages contain questions designed to help you complete the step, together with two additional pages for any further questions your sponsor would like you to consider before you both agree that you are ready to move on to the next step.

The Step 4 section of this Workbook is brief and is not intended to replace the full contained in your own fellowship's literature. If you need further assistance with Step 4, you may find my 4th Step Workbook helpful. It is available at: www.amazon.com/dp/1798709953.

GRATITUDE LIST

I recommend adding at least 5 items to a gratitude list every day.

Being grateful will help motivate you as you work the steps, as well as building emotional resilience you can draw on during challenging times in your recovery.

JOURNAL PAGES

You can use the journal for many purposes. Here are some examples:

- Journal about your day;
- Journal your feelings;
- Writing affirmations;
- Step 10 daily inventory;
- List recovery actions taken: daily reading, step work, meeting attended, outreach calls, prayer and meditation, 12th step work undertaken.

12 STEP WORKBOOK SECTION

STEP 1

We admitted we were powerless over our addiction/others - that our lives had become unmanageable.

If you are ready, it's time to take a long hard look at your PROBLEM - the negative behaviors caused by your addiction/codependency - and the impact it has had on your own life as well as the lives of those around you.

To take this Step, we recommend you read your fellowship's 12-step literature, attend step meetings, talk to your Sponsor, and only when you have done all that, write out answers to these questions. All these actions together, will allow you to see the TRUTH about your problem close up.

All you need to complete this process is the WILLINGNESS to be HONEST.

Once you have completed the questions, you will have taken Step 1. You will fully recognize your powerlessness over your addiction, and your inability to control your life and behaviour through self-will alone. This is the process of surrender,, and it is the first step to recovery.

Only by admitting defeat will you be ready and willing to move on to Step 2, which introduces you to the solution.

List the actions you have already taken and literature you have read to aid you in working this step.

What does powerlessness mean to you today?

What characteristics or behaviours prevent you from taking Step 1?

_____

_____

_____

_____

_____

_____

_____

_____

_____

_____

_____

_____

_____

_____

_____

_____

_____

_____

_____

_____

Write 10 ways your addiction / codependency makes your life unmanageable.

Why does this step say "we were powerless" not I was powerless?

Write 10 ways you tried to control your addiction / other people.

What is the specific reason you came into recovery?

_____

_____

_____

_____

_____

_____

_____

_____

_____

_____

_____

_____

_____

_____

_____

_____

_____

_____

_____

_____

How has your addiction / codependency affected your health?

How has your addiction diminished your life?

How have your relationships been affected by your addiction / codependency?

Step 1 questions from your sponsor.

Step 1 questions from your sponsor.

Step 1 questions from your sponsor.

_____

_____

_____

_____

_____

_____

_____

_____

_____

_____

_____

_____

_____

_____

_____

_____

_____

_____

_____

Step 1 questions from your sponsor.

STEP 2

Came to believe that a Power greater than ourselves could restore us to sanity.

After learning about your PROBLEM, Step 2 brings HOPE by introducing the SOLUTION. Step 2's message is that, while you are powerless over your addiction,, a Power greater than your own self-will can *"restore you to sanity"*.

You may already have faith in a spiritual Higher Power, or you may, like me, never fully develop one you are ready to trust. It doesn't matter. This step asks only that you BELIEVE that there is a Power which can help you overcome your problem of addiction, not that you to believe in any specific God, or indeed any God at all.

In fact, where the Steps are concerned, believing in a spiritual God of your understanding can be more challenging than believing that the 12-steps which have worked for millions of people already, will be more successful in tackling the disease of addiction than your self-will alone.

And please don't worry about the words "restore you to sanity", remember the definition of sanity: *"being able to think and behave in a reasonable and rational manner"*. No doubt we can agree we have, at times, all lacked this ability when it came to our addictions /codependency.

List the actions you have already taken and literature you have read to prepare you for this step.

Do you believe you need a 'power' to help you with your addiction / codependence?

_____

_____

_____

_____

_____

_____

_____

_____

_____

_____

_____

_____

_____

_____

_____

_____

_____

_____

_____

_____

_____

What are your fears and prejudices that are preventing you from finding a power greater than yourself?

How do pride, ego and shame stand in the way of you asking for help?

What actions are you willing to take to find your Higher Power?

What does "Came to believe" mean to you?

What does sanity mean to you today?

What does restore us to sanity mean in the context of Step 2?

How would you describe the experience of having a Higher Power in your life?

Give examples of things you can barely believe you did in active addiction.

How has my belief in a higher power changed since I came into recovery?

What parts of my life do I have hope about today?

Step 2 questions from your sponsor.

Step 2 questions from your sponsor.

STEP 3

Made a decision to turn our will
and our lives over to the care of
God as we understood God.

Having taken Steps 1 and 2, you should now realize that you have been powerless over your addiction/codependency, and that the solution to your problem is to get help from something more powerful than your own self-will alone, whether that is a God of your understanding or your 12 step program and the people in it.

Step 3 asks you to make a decision that when the voice of your addiction is whispering in your ear, you will allow your Higher Power to guide you on the path of recovery. If you have faith in God, this is where you turn your will and life over through prayer. If you are using the 12 step program as your Higher Power, this may simply mean that you commit to using the tools of the program.

In this step you decide to have FAITH that, even though self-will has failed you in the past, your Higher Power will not. Every time you are tempted to act on your addiction/codependency, you turn to your Higher Power (either God or the program) for support and guidance.

The trick is to make the decision to turn your life over to God, in the moment – moment by moment – every day until this reliance on something other than your addictive thinking, becomes as natural as breathing. It is only through habit that the voice of recovery becomes louder than the voice of your addiction.

List the actions you have already taken and literature you have read to prepare you for this step.

_____

_____

_____

_____

_____

_____

_____

_____

_____

_____

_____

_____

_____

_____

_____

_____

_____

_____

_____

_____

What does the step ask of us when it states 'Made a Decision'.

What does "turning over" mean to you?

What does "my will and my life" mean in the context of Step 3?

In what ways does self-will give you an illusion of control or power?

In what ways is willingness the key to Step 3?

Why is a life based on self-sufficiency not sufficient for you to recover from your addiction / codependency?

_____

_____

_____

_____

_____

_____

_____

_____

_____

_____

_____

_____

_____

_____

_____

_____

_____

_____

_____

_____

Are you still trying to handle your problems yourself or are you asking for help?

Write a list of benefits you would receive if you relied on a higher power.

What character defects are still preventing you from relying on a higher power?

In what ways are you willing to practice 'Letting go and letting god'?

Give examples of times when your own self-will alone has not been enough.

_____

_____

_____

_____

_____

_____

_____

_____

_____

_____

_____

_____

_____

_____

_____

_____

_____

_____

_____

_____

_____

_____

Step 3 questions from your sponsor.

Step 3 questions from your sponsor.

STEP 4

Made a searching and
fearless moral inventory of
ourselves.

Step 4 is a step of COURAGE. Before you began working the program, the voice of your addiction was far more alluring (and eventually irresistible) than the voice of recovery. You reacted to anger, resentments, fears, and shame from the past by succumbing to your addictions.

In Step 4 you face up to what you have done and who you have become – a person you could not face without resorting to addictive behaviour. You begin the process of transforming yourself into someone who can live a happy life, without the need to resort to addictive behaviors.

Step 4 is a major endeavor, and it must be undertaken thoroughly, if you are to move easily through the remaining steps. We recommend you write your Step 4 inventory in one of the three following ways: write a life story; follow the "columns" method; or answer detailed questions designed to extract a thorough inventory of your life.

If you choose the third option, you may want to use my Step 4 Workbook, which you can find here: www.amazon.com//dp/1798709953.

And remember, the questions in this workbook are **not a substitute** for an in-depth Step 4, they are designed to give you an insight into the process of inventorying your life.

List the actions you have already taken and literature you have read to prepare you for this step.

What reservations do you have about taking Step 4?

What does "fearless" mean to you?

What do you understand "moral inventory" to mean?

_____

_____

_____

_____

_____

_____

_____

_____

_____

_____

_____

_____

_____

_____

_____

_____

_____

_____

_____

_____

_____

Have you stolen from people or institutions?

What non-material things have you stolen?

Do you gossip about others? Why do you do this and how does it make you feel?

Do you put unreasonable expectations on others? How?

Do you judge others or make fun of them? Why?

Do you feel misunderstood or unappreciated? How?

In what ways do you feel superior or inferior to others?

List 10 resentments you have carried with you in your daily life.

List 10 people you have harmed and state how.

How has fear impacted your life?

In what ways have you hurt others through your sex conduct?

_____

_____

_____

_____

_____

_____

_____

_____

_____

_____

_____

_____

_____

_____

_____

_____

_____

_____

_____

How does undertaking Step 4 help you to see yourself as you truly are?

What are your values? What is important to you?

What people or institutions do you resent? Why?

How has your own behaviour contributed to these resentments?

What feelings do you have trouble feeling? Why?

Step 4 questions from your sponsor.

Step 4 questions from your sponsor.

STEP 5

Admitted to God, to ourselves
and to another human being
the exact nature of our
wrongs.

"You're as sick as your secrets." That is what you are told when you come into recovery. If you are to live a life of INTEGRITY, you must use Step 5 to shine a light into the darkness or those secrets. Step 5 takes the power out of your shameful, painful or downright criminal behaviors by bringing them out into the open.

Sharing your story with your Sponsor can also help you identify patterns of behaviour and character defects which have led to unwanted behaviors. When you come across these characteristics, write them down; you'll need a list when you begin working Steps 6 and 7. And while you're writing lists, why not use Step 5 to start listing the people you have harmed through your addiction. You'll need that in Steps 8 and 9.

But what of sharing it with God you ask? If you have a belief in God, please go ahead and find a way to share with that Power in a way that feels right for you. You may want to share it with a priest or minister, spiritual adviser or just find a peaceful place in nature and read your Step 4 out loud.

If, like me, you don't believe in God, and are using the program as your Higher Power, the act of sharing the contents of your Step 4 with a person in the program (normally a Sponsor), will be enough.

List the actions you have already taken and literature you have read to prepare you for this step.

_____

_____

_____

_____

_____

_____

_____

_____

_____

_____

_____

_____

_____

_____

_____

_____

_____

_____

_____

Why is Step 5 so frightening?

How can you work through your fears about Step 5?

_____

_____

_____

_____

_____

_____

_____

_____

_____

_____

_____

_____

_____

_____

_____

_____

_____

_____

_____

_____

_____

What does admitting the exact nature of your wrongs mean to you?

How will you share this Step with you Higher Power?

How will you develop trust with the person you plan to share this step
with?

What expectations do I have of the person I choose to share Step 5 with?

_____

_____

_____

_____

_____

_____

_____

_____

_____

_____

_____

_____

_____

_____

_____

_____

_____

_____

_____

_____

Write down the names of the two people you are closest to.

Next to the names from the previous page, write two negative and two positive feelings you have towards them.

If you feel you have harmed the people on the previous list, how will you forgive yourself?

What is the differents between listing your wrongs and admitting the exact nature of your wrongs?

Do you believe working this step will improve your life? How?

After sharing your Step 4, what have you learned about yourself?

Have your feelings about yourself changed through practicing Step 5?

Step 5 questions from your sponsor.

Step 5 questions from your sponsor.

STEP 6

Were entirely ready to have God remove all these defects of character.

Having begun the process of bringing your past into the light, you now move to Step 6, which is a step of WILLINGNESS.

Begin by identifying the defects of character that stand in the way of your recovery transformation. How? Working from your Step 4 inventory, write a comprehensive list of the defects which you feel are blocking you from living a happy life: were you arrogant or grandiose, self-centered or proud? These are the behaviors and characteristics, that when left unchecked, caused you to revert to your addictive ways.

When listing your character defects, it is also important to list the personality traits that are helping you in your life and your recovery journey. It is all too easy, when working Steps 6 and 7, to focus solely on the negative and forget that you have many positive attributes, and that your defects do not define you.

In my experience, the act of recognizing and listing these defects takes you a long way along the path of willingness to let go of them.

The questions in this section are designed to help you reach the stage of being entirely ready to have your Higher Power (the program) remove them.

List the actions you have already taken and literature you have read to prepare you for this step.

When you have completed your Step 5 with a sponsor, write a list of recurring character defects.

Why is Step 6 necessary?

How do you feel about the phrase "defects of character"? Why?

Are you afraid that without some of your defects you will become boring? Why?

Do you truly believe you cannot remove these defects without help?
Why?

How will you become "entirely ready" to have your Higher Power removed your defects?

_____

_____

_____

_____

_____

_____

_____

_____

_____

_____

_____

_____

_____

_____

_____

_____

_____

_____

Which character defects are you willing to release right now?

Which character defects are you not yet ready to have removed?

What are the negative consequences of the defects from your list?

Do you have any defects you think cannot be removed? Why?

What actions can you take to show you are entirely ready?

How will you know when you are ready to move to Step 7?

Step 6 questions from your sponsor.

Step 6 questions from your sponsor.

STEP 7

Humbly asked God to
remove our shortcomings.

In Step 6 you identified your shortcomings and became willing to let them go. Now, in Step 7 you use prayer and meditation to ask your Higher Power (whether that is God or the program) to remove each of these defects of character. This step requires HUMILITY as you are asked, once again, to admit you cannot remove these defects without help.

But that's not all. As they say, "nature abhors a vacuum", so in step 7 you need to take action yourself. Whenever you find yourself about to act in an unwanted way, you use the knowledge you have found in the program to take a different action. A good way of changing an action is by consciously replacing the unwanted behaviour with a different, opposite, behaviour.

For example, if you want to stop being selfish and self-centered, you can actively work on being kind and considerate. It is only through filling the gap your Higher Power has created by removing the shortcoming with a different action or behaviour, that you will prevent the old defect from returning.

The following questions aim to help you to work through Step 7 and in doing so, become ready to move on to Step 8, where you begin the process of making amends to those you have harmed.

List the actions you have already taken and literature you have read to prepare you for this step.

What do you understand the words humble and humilty mean to you?

What do you understand the word shortcomings to mean?

What do you fear you will lose if your shortcomings are removed?

How has working the previous steps helped you work Step 7?

_____

_____

_____

_____

_____

_____

_____

_____

_____

_____

_____

_____

_____

_____

_____

_____

_____

_____

_____

_____

_____

What will you receive if your shortcomings are removed?

Describe your positive qualities - the person you could be all the time if your shorcomings were removed.

_____

_____

_____

_____

_____

_____

_____

_____

_____

_____

_____

_____

_____

_____

_____

_____

_____

_____

_____

On your list of defects from Step 6, write the positive quality you consider the opposite of each defect.

How can you develop these positive qualities in your life, to take the place of the shortcomings you wish to be removed?

How can you surrender and release self-will in relation to Step 7?

At the end of Step 7, which shortcomings have been removed or diminished in my life?

_____

_____

_____

_____

_____

_____

_____

_____

_____

_____

_____

_____

_____

_____

_____

_____

_____

_____

_____

Step 7 questions from your sponsor.

Step 7 questions from your sponsor.

STEP 8

Made a list of all persons we had harmed, and became willing to make amends to them all.

Step 8 is where you take RESPONSIBILITY for your actions.

In Step 5, you or your Sponsor, made a list of the people and institutions you harmed (as well as how you harmed them). Here, in Step 8, you take the time to add any names that you feel should also be on the list.

With the complete list in front of you, it is time to become WILLING to make amends to all these people and institutions.

Many people choose to split the list into three: those they are ready to make amends to now; those to whom they are not yet not ready to make amends, but believe they will be willing; and those they can't see themselves ever being willing to make amends to. Splitting the list in this way will enable you to get started on Step 9 with the first list, while still working on your willingness with the other lists.

The following questions are designed to help you become WILLING to make amends, so that you can move on to Step 9.

List the actions you have already taken and literature you have read to prepare you for this step.

Using your Step 4 inventory write a list of all persons you have harmed.

_____

_____

_____

_____

_____

_____

_____

_____

_____

_____

_____

_____

_____

_____

_____

_____

_____

_____

_____

_____

_____

Add any names you think should be on this list but were not in your Step 4 inventory.

Write the way in which you harmed each of these people next to their name.

Can you identify any patterns of harms you have done? What are they?

Make a List of the resentments that stand in the way of you taking this Step.

_____

_____

_____

_____

_____

_____

_____

_____

_____

_____

_____

_____

_____

_____

_____

_____

_____

_____

_____

_____

_____

_____

About who do you still feel fearful or defensive?

Who are you already willing to make amends to?

Who are you not yet willing to make amends to? Include people you do not feel you will ever be able to make amends to.

How will you become willing?

Do you have any financial amends to make to people?

Do I owe any amends to people who have harmed me? How will I separate the two when making amends?

How will you forgive yourself?

What emotional (and other) harm have you done to yourself?

Why is saying sorry not sufficient to repair the damage you caused?

Step 8 questions from your sponsor.

Step 8 questions from your sponsor.

STEP 9

Made direct amends to such people wherever possible, except when to do so would injure them or others.

By now you will have a list (or several) of names of people (and institutions) you need to make amends to. And after Step 8, you should now be ready to make amends to at least some of them. It takes DISCIPLINE to face the people you have harmed.

The questions in this section should help you in making amends, but you will also need to talk through the process with your Sponsor to decide what form the amends should take in each case and how you should go about making them. There are many ways to make amends and you should ask for guidance from your Higher Power, your sponsor and/or your spiritual adviser when deciding how to proceed. Some examples of amends you might make are financial restitution or an apology coupled by changing your behaviour going forward.

If you are hesitant to move forward with this step, remember that your guilt and remorse, coupled with your resentments and fears, are what is holding you back from the total transformation you are working towards.

Remember, you should not make amends to people if it would cause harm to them or other people, and when making an amend, you must always take care of your own emotional, mental and physical wellbeing before proceeding.

List the actions you have already taken and literature you have read to prepare you for this step.

_____

_____

_____

_____

_____

_____

_____

_____

_____

_____

_____

_____

_____

_____

_____

_____

_____

_____

_____

What does the word amends mean to you?

Why does this step specify "direct amends"?

_____

_____

_____

_____

_____

_____

_____

_____

_____

_____

_____

_____

_____

_____

_____

_____

_____

_____

_____

_____

_____

What can you do if direct amends are not possible?

_____

_____

_____

_____

_____

_____

_____

_____

_____

_____

_____

_____

_____

_____

_____

_____

_____

_____

_____

_____

_____

_____

What do you believe to be the purpose of making amends?

How will you prepare to make amends?

_____

_____

_____

_____

_____

_____

_____

_____

_____

_____

_____

_____

_____

_____

_____

_____

_____

_____

_____

_____

How can you take care of yourself emotionally (and in other ways) when making amends?

Make a list of people you are willing to make amends to but cannot because it would injure them or others.

Write down how you plan to make amends to each name on your list and discuss with your sponsor.

How will you make amends to yourself?

In what way is "making amends" different from saying you are sorry?

_____

_____

_____

_____

_____

_____

_____

_____

_____

_____

_____

_____

_____

_____

_____

_____

_____

_____

_____

Why is it not important how your amends are received?

Have you forgiven the people who have harmed you?

To which names on your amends list can you not make a direct or of indirect amends at all? Why?

_____

_____

_____

_____

_____

_____

_____

_____

_____

_____

_____

_____

_____

_____

_____

_____

_____

_____

_____

_____

Can I still make some form of amend to this person, or change my behaviour? How?

How did it feel to make amends? What did you learn about yourself through this step?

Step 9 questions from your sponsor.

Step 9 questions from your sponsor.

STEP 10

Continued to take personal
inventory and when we were wrong
promptly admitted it.

By now, you have gone a long way towards clearing the wreckage of your past. You have taken inventory, worked on your defects of character and made amends to those you have harmed (or at least some of them). Hopefully, you will now feel less shame and guilt and be more able to live your life in a more balanced, healthy way.

The purpose of Step 10 is twofold. Firstly, it allows you to clean house on an ongoing basis by picking up on unwanted behaviour and making immediate amends if that behaviour harms others.

Secondly, (and this is easy to forget) writing a daily Step 10 gives you the opportunity to study your behaviour patterns over the long term. Are you rude to your spouse or work colleagues when you are overtired or hungry? Are you grandiose or condescending? Keeping and reviewing a daily Step 10 is an effective way to pick up on the more subtle character defects, which raise their heads after you have dealt with the worst ones. What's more, it will help guard against going back to character defects you have already dealt with.

Remember, when you ask for your character defects to be removed, you also need to put in the legwork by fostering another behaviour (usually the opposite) in its place.

List the actions you have already taken and literature you have read to prepare you for this step.

_____

_____

_____

_____

_____

_____

_____

_____

_____

_____

_____

_____

_____

_____

_____

_____

_____

_____

_____

_____

What do you understand to be the purpose of this step?

What do you understand 'wongs' to be in the context of Step 10?

How does admiting my wrongs help me to change my behaviour?

What are the benefits of writing a daily inventory?

Why do you repeat the same behaviours and what can you learn from doing Step 10?

_____

_____

_____

_____

_____

_____

_____

_____

_____

_____

_____

_____

_____

_____

_____

_____

_____

_____

How does this step help you to live in the present?

Step 10 Inventory: List times when you have been afraid, angry, resentful, controlling and ashamed today?

Step 10 Inventory: How did any of your character defects flare up today?

Step 10 Inventory: Which, if any, of your actions require you to make amends?

Step 10 Inventory: What did you do well / differently than you would have done prior to recovery?

Step 10 inventory: List the feelings you had today.

Why is it important to include positive changes in this inventory?

In what ways do you understand gratitude to be part of this step?

How does Step 10 help me to live in the present moment?

Step 10 questions from your sponsor.

Step 10 questions from your sponsor.

STEP 11

Sought through prayer and meditation to improve our conscious contact with God as we understood God, praying only for knowledge of God's will for us and the power to carry that out.

Step 11 talks about prayer and meditation to improve your conscious contact with your Higher Power. If you have a spiritual God that is your Higher Power, you will already know how to pray to that God. If the program is your Higher Power, you can use prayer as a way of reconfirming the HUMILITY and WILLINGNESS to continue working the program of recovery you learned in the earlier steps.

Thoughts are powerful. If you regularly pray and direct your thoughts towards bringing your life into alignment with the principles of the program (which is the will of your Higher Power), simply by bringing that intention into your consciousness, you will begin to express those qualities in your daily life.

When you practice meditation, you are getting to know your higher-self - what some of us would call our soul or spirit - while also building a connection with your Higher Power. By understanding and becoming aware of your deepest wants and needs, you connect with what your Higher Power wants for you. At its simplest, this is freedom from our addictions.

List the actions you have already taken and literature you have read to prepare you for this step.

_____

_____

_____

_____

_____

_____

_____

_____

_____

_____

_____

_____

_____

_____

_____

_____

_____

_____

_____

What do you think is the purpose of Step 11?

How do you feel about praying? How do you feel about meditating?

What do the words "improve my conscious contact" mean to you?

In what ways have you taken your will back from your Higher Power?

How does gratitude help you connect with your Higher Power?

Why does this step focus on your Higher Power's will for you and not what you personally want?

Why is it important to spend daily quiet time alone?

Write down the ways you practice prayer and meditation?

How can you use Step 11 in challenging times?

What is your vision of your higher power's will for you?

Why do you only ask for knowledge of God's will for you and the power to carry it out?

Have I been given what I need? What are some of the things you have received?

_____

_____

_____

_____

_____

_____

_____

_____

_____

_____

_____

_____

_____

_____

_____

_____

_____

_____

_____

Step 11 questions from your sponsor.

Step 11 questions from your sponsor.

STEP 12

Having had a spiritual awakening as the result of these steps, we tried to carry this message to other addicts/codependents, and to practice these principles in all our affairs.

By the time you reach Step 12 you will have cleared the wreckage of the past, changed your unwanted behaviors, and connected with a deep understanding of your life in recovery. This transformation is what the program refers to as a spiritual awakening.

Being convinced that you have experienced this transformation as a result of the program, you will feel compelled to carry the message of recovery to others. In gratitude for the freedom you have been given by the program, you begin to give SERVICE to others.

Not everyone is suited to every type of service. We suggest that you try any or all of the following: service at meetings, answering a helpline, going on "12 step calls" to newcomers, helping at area or district meetings. You don't have to do everything but it is recommended that you have at least one service position at any time, to help keep you connected to the fellowship and focused on helping others.

This is the second benefit to "carrying the message to others" which is that while you are helping others you are taken out of yourself, and thus less likely to act on our addictive impulses. By being of service and sponsoring others we are better placed to "give it away to keep it".

List the actions you have already taken and literature you have read to prepare you for this step.

If a Spiritual Awakening is defined as total transformation, how have you been transformed while working the steps?

Have you had a spiritual awakening as the result of these steps? How can you tell?

_____

_____

_____

_____

_____

_____

_____

_____

_____

_____

_____

_____

_____

_____

_____

_____

_____

_____

_____

_____

_____

List some of the miracles of your recovery so far.

What is the message of recovery that you can carry to others?

List the ways you could carry the message to others.

What benefits does doing service give back to you?

What do you think "these principles" means in the context of Step 12?

What part has 12th Step work played in your recovery? What more could you do?

Which principles of the program do you find it hardest to practice?

What are my feelings about service to others?

What are you doing right now to maintain your recovery?

Step 12 questions from your sponsor.

Step 12 questions from your sponsor.

GRATITUDE LIST

Gratitude List:

Gratitude List continued:

Gratitude List continued:

Gratitude List continued:

JOURNAL

Made in the USA
Monee, IL
02 June 2023

35158343R00136